Victory Psalms

Volume 1

By Wes Palmer

This book is dedicated to my wonderful Lord and Savior: Jesus Christ. Also, to my fine, Christian wife: Gay Barbara.

Information

Information

If you have comments or questions, you can reach me at
the following email address:

wesleypalmer2018@gmail.com

Table of Contents

Introduction

My name is Wes Palmer and I was born in Amery, Wisconsin. My parents moved the family to Minnesota around 1950 and we took up residence just two blocks away from a local church. Being brought to church regularly during childhood was very important for me considering the struggle that was to take place in my life in the years to come. Crying spells and fear was the bread of my formative years. After going to college for two years, getting married and having three children, fear, depression and psychosis covered me like a dark cloud. Then in the fall of 1983, I ended up in a padded cell beating my head against the wall because I was overcome by the stress and confusion. Behind the scenes in all of this, my future Lord and Savior, Jesus Christ, was working His marvelous will for me by delivering me from all that I suffered from into His great goodness. First of all, I had godly parents who lived the Christian life before me as best as they knew how. Secondly, I accepted Jesus as my Lord and Savior when I was 21 years old. Thirdly, my future wife became a Christian right before my eyes in the church I attended on the night I first met her. Finally, I received the baptism of the Holy Spirit in 1976. From the padded cell until now, after spending a year and a half in a group home away from family, the Lord has continued to restore my mind and family as I put my trust in Him.

Out of the furnace of past afflictions, the Lord has blessed me with Victory Psalms that tell of His past, present and future work in my life for His glory to deliver me from the jaws of defeat into complete victory. From the psalms in this book, the psalm called, "Victory Song" beams forth the light of God's mercy and how He strengthened and changed me forever.

> *My heart is pure, conscience is clear, I have great understanding*
> *The mind of Christ, an iron will and godly emotions*
> *A strong and healthy body for all of my days*

I thank you, Lord, for the victory

The "Eternity" psalm I wrote expresses the eternal hope I have in Jesus and what it means to me in my inner most being.

Eternity, eternity, everything pales beside it
Never-ending, never ceasing, time without end
When all is said and over, it's the relationship that gets it done
Walking in victory with the ever-living Son

In the "Heaven" psalm I rest my thoughts on the glory that is to come.

In heaven there is nothing to diminish the glory of God
Poverty, sickness and spiritual death are earthly things that will be gone
The enemy has been banished, the curse will be no more
Complete fulfillment comes to us when we walk on heaven's gold
After the 1,000 year reign of Christ, heaven will come down here
God will enjoy his family for the rest of eternity

My "You've Rescued Me" psalm binds together all these things in the Victory of the cross.

O, Lord, you've rescued me, from the darkness you let me see
Your Word renews my mind, lights the path that I can find
Your Spirit comforts my heart, and nothing can keep us apart

Your love is now mine to share for all time, you've given the sign

The writings contained in this book can be recited as poems, sung and also used for confessions to strengthen, encourage and comfort you in line with the Word of God. These psalms testify to the victory we have in Jesus over all the power of the enemy and I hope these psalms encourage you as much as I have been encouraged in living and writing them.

"And the God of all grace, who called you to his eternal glory in Christ, after you have suffered a little while, will himself restore you and make you strong, firm and steadfast. To him be the power for ever and ever. Amen." (1 Peter 5:10–11)

Psalm 1 : A New Song

To the churches of believers, listen to what the Spirit says
Repent and be victorious even unto death
Then you can eat from the Tree of Life
In the presence of our Savior, the Lord Jesus Christ

Repent and be victorious, the second death will not harm you
Repent and be victorious and you will rule the nations
Receive the hidden manna and a new name
Listen, listen, listen to what the Spirit says

Repent and be victorious to be dressed in white
Acknowledged before the Father, never erased from the Book of Life
Repent and be victorious a pillar in the house of God
Repent and be victorious sit with Jesus on his throne

To the churches of believers, listen to what the Spirit says
Victory in Jesus each and every day
Victory in Jesus, this is the godly lifestyle
Then, be welcomed into the kingdom without any guile

Listen, listen, listen to what the Spirit says
Repent and be victorious even unto death
Then you can eat from the Tree of Life
In the presence of our Savior the Lord Jesus Christ
In the paradise of Heaven far above all sin and strife

Psalm 2 : Apostles of Victory

We are apostles of victory
Overcoming all adversity
With faith, hope and love
Yes, every good gift from above
Sent forth to minister
As the Spirit leads
Not in defeat
Or ever in retreat

We are apostles of victory
Just like Jesus
With his full armor on
Enemies we tread upon
To further the Kingdom of God
Advancing on every front
Preaching repentance to all in the name of the Son

We are apostles of victory
Redeemed from the curse
Discipling others
Like a loving, heavenly nurse
An example to neighbors
In all our family labors
Our testimony lines up with the Word
Walking in victory as we serve

Psalm 3 : As the Spirit Leads

Led by the Spirit
Not by the clock or reason
Ministering unto others
In the proper due season
Not by rule or formula
Following Jesus fully
Edifying and blessing
Come about so truly

Acknowledging Him in all our ways
The Spirit will lead us
Bringing hope and encouragement
Strength and comfort to please us
Always in line with the Word
In the fear of the Lord
Serving others with love and respect
Without any neglect
Serving others with love and respect
Without any neglect

Psalm 4 : Authority Song

One thing we must understand: the believer's authority
After making the faith command, we stand in victory
The Father blesses us to our account
When we offer the prayer of faith without any doubt

Before his Ascension Jesus said these words:
Preach and make disciples
As you go into all the world
Signs shall follow as you use my Name
Sharing the Good News which you must proclaim

Resist the devil with the shield of faith
He will flee from our presence leaving no trace
As we take captive every wayward thought
Demolishing strongholds is one thing Jesus for us bought

As New Testament saints to his authority we must cling
Using every weapon in the arsenal of our King
Enforcing the victory wherever He tells us to go
Soldiers in the army of the living Lord

One thing we now understand
The believer's authority in our hand
As we speak darkness scatters
This is what really matters
Enforcing the victory wherever He tells us to go
Soldiers in the army of the living Lord

Psalm 5 : Because of Your Great Love

Jesus, Jesus, God came down to my level
Put on flesh to pass the ultimate test
Jesus, Jesus, lost everything for my gain
Life, position and power; this was the Great Exchange

Loving Master, the Martyr was He
Faced the fire meant for me
Lived and died, his sacrifice
Rose from the dead brought about eternal life

Jesus, Jesus, worshipping you in spirit
Satisfies all of my heart cries
Jesus, Jesus, picture of perfection
My Hero, my Hero, my holy selection

Suffered sin's penalty
Righteousness imputed unto me
The fullness of God inside of me
All this happened to transform me

Jesus, Jesus, redeemed me from the curse
Into your mercy wholly immersed
Jesus, Jesus there is no end to your kindness
All because of your great love
You removed man's blindness
All because of your great love
You removed man's blindness

Psalm 6 : Blood Covenant

Ordained by God the shedding of blood
After the Fall, it was shed for man's covering
God made covenant with Abraham
A blood-sworn oath settled the plan
The life of the flesh is in the blood

Once blood was shed no turning back
A solemn vow enforced the covenant
At the first Passover lambs were slain
Blood was applied to keep the destroyer away

Sacrificial system set up to cover sin
Fellowship was established through the Old Covenant
From fresh to tradition to mechanical routine
The first testament just covered sin

At the perfect time God sent his Son
For the establishment of the New Covenant
Most precious substance the blood of Christ
Eternal redemption to bring us life

Once and for all sacrifice has been made
The New Covenant will never pass away
Remission of sin to make us holy
Received by faith it is the way only

Honor the blood don't ever turn away
The most sacred sacrifice has been made
Don't profane the blood of Christ
Don't ever spit in the cup of life

Ordained by God the shedding of blood
At the perfect time God sent his Son
Honor the blood don't ever turn away
The most sacred sacrifice has been made

Psalm 7 : Cast out Fear

What did Jesus say?
He said: "Do not be afraid!"
Casting out all fear
Because perfect love is here

Fear is tormenting
But God He is our peace
Speak the Word of God from your heart
And experience a great release

Trusting in the Lord
Living by faith
Believing in Him you cannot see
You're blessed with victory

Fear came upon mankind
In the garden of Eden
But Jesus redeemed us from the curse
Brought rest unto his church

In the New Covenant
Faith is the key
Casting out all fear
Because perfect love is here

Trusting in the Lord
Living by faith
Believing in Him you cannot see
Brings blessed victory

Summing it all up
Jesus drank from the cup
Became the author of our faith
Fear has been replaced
In the New Covenant faith is the key
Casting out all fear because perfect love is here

Psalm 8 : Choose Life

Words of faith, words of love, words of victory from above
Speaking out good things pleases God as we travel this earthly sod
The mouth is used, not for strife, my tongue only chooses life

I only speak in line with the Word

Uttering the truth in love, giving thanks and giving praise
Blessing the Lord with all my heart, from out of my inner, inner part
Building up others, edifying, this is my way of testifying

Only good things come out of my mouth

I speak only the Word of God, what I hear my Father say
Jesus brings, brings to pass, the good that comes out of my lips
I bridle my tongue by the Spirit today, keeping perverseness far away

The Lord dictates what I say

I choose faith, I choose faith, I choose faith instead of fear
I choose hope, I choose hope, I choose hope and not despair
I choose love, I choose love, I choose love instead of hate

I only speak in line with the Word
Only good things come out of my mouth
The Lord dictates what I say

Yes, I choose life, I choose life, I choose life instead of death
I choose life, I choose life, I choose life instead of death
I choose life, I choose life, I choose life instead of death

Psalm 9 : Communion

Solemn, sober and serious
We dedicate ourselves to you
As we eat the bread, we drink the cup
Deeply remember as we sup
The Lord's death in our consciousness
Until He returns in line with the Word
We examine and judge ourselves
Discerning the body of Christ Himself
Not condemned with this old world
But staying strong and healthy for all of our days
For our God He never fails

Psalm 10 : Concepts of Victory

Fill up your heart with the Word of God, meditate on it fully
Revelation knowledge will come to you, as you walk in love
Faith is growing exceedingly, as we hear and digest the Word
Working by love, victory from above, manifested in your life

Just like Jesus in this world, compassion controls us
Through our every word and deed, the Father fills all we need

As we wait upon El Shaddai, nothing missing or broken
With every godly request, the answer is yes
He is our promise provider

Provision is to be a blessing, coming from out of our heart
First to our family, others as the Spirit leads

An intimate relationship with our God, we are one with Him
Never forsaken or cast aside, from his love we cannot hide

Fill up your heart with the Word of God, meditate on it fully
Revelation knowledge will come to you, as you walk in love
Faith is growing exceedingly, as we hear and digest the Word
Working by love, victory from above, manifested in your life
Working by love, victory from above, manifested in your life

Psalm 11 : Discipling

Make disciples of the nations
Training people from all generations
Teaching from the Word of the Lord
With the Spirit in one accord

Believers be an example to others
In thought, word and deed
Showing what it is like
To be a Jesus for all to see

What a change of pace
Being trained without haste
In church and out of church
Discipled in our Bible search

Formally taught voluntarily
Setting aside time every week
A point of contact is good for the soul
Part of the process to be made whole

One-on-one can't be beat
The mentor and the trainee with the Lord to meet
Walking in victory is one of the goals

So make disciples of the nations
Training people from all generations
Teaching from the Word of the Lord
With the Spirit in one accord

Psalm 12 : Done with Fear

I was ravaged by fearful thoughts through the course of time
The shield of faith with my spoken words stopped the sharp attacks
No longer unarmed, I have the full armor of God on
I now have the victory over all the power of the enemy

With the name of Jesus and faith in Him
In the race set before us triumph is our theme
We are blessed and always on top
Our journey with Christ it will never stop

Confident and courageous like Daniel in the den
There is no place for fearful thinking in our walk of patient faith
For our focus is always on God's loving face
His Word, his presence in our lives gives the devil no place

The promptings of the Spirit must be acted on
To keep rivers flowing in the inner man
Streams of living water flooding within
Refreshment from the fountain no more consciousness of sin

I was ravaged by fearful thoughts through the course of time
The shield of faith with my spoken words stopped the sharp attacks
No longer unarmed, I have the full armor of God on
I now have the victory over all the power of the enemy
I now have the victory over all the power of the enemy

Psalm 13 : Eternity

Eternity, eternity, everything pales beside it
The choice you make in this world is crucial to your future inside it
Everlasting life with Jesus or with the cruel, godless enemy
Yes, life with the loving Jesus or Satan our adversary

All conceived in this earth will never cease to exist
It pleased the Father of spirits to put us on his list
Listen carefully to what you hear, your destiny awaits
What's in your heart so near out of the mouth determines your fate

Eternity, eternity, everything pales beside it
Never-ending, never ceasing, time without end
When all is said and over, it's the relationship that gets it done
Walking in victory with the ever-living Son

Our long, full lifespan prepares us for what's ahead
Filled with the fruit of the Spirit, faith and patience bring it to pass
Now redeemed from the curse of the law,
    on earth we have been blessed
Then, eternity in heaven, when Jesus comes back again

Eternity, eternity, everything pales beside it
The choice you make in this world is crucial to your future inside it
Everlasting life with Jesus or with the cruel, godless enemy
Choose life with the loving Jesus for the rest of eternity

Psalm 14 : Faith Song

According to your faith so be it done unto you
As you have believed it shall come true
Receive what you speak out
With this law there is no doubt
The faith coming out of your mouth is what it's about

Words acquit or condemn
They can justify in the end
Bring blessing or cursing
Invite the Spirit's immersing
Shout out the victory
Praising God continually

Faith is the victory that overcomes the world
It ever-grows by love unfurled
Both spring from hope stored up above
It's our responsibility to keep our faith strong and lean

We have the solid rock to stand upon
Jesus Christ the righteous one
Fixed and established in our talk
He's the developer of our faith walk

As our thoughts, words and deeds lineup
We feast at His table where we sup
Troubles come this is for sure
But faith is the victory that overcomes the world
Faith is the victory that overcomes the world

Psalm 15 : Fill Me Up

Fill me up, fill me up, fill me up with thy goodness, O, Lord
So, fill me up, fill me up, fill me up with thy goodness, O, Lord

Teach me thy statutes in my heart
Give me peace and joy as I carry on
Thank you for the Spirit, O, Lord

Thank you for the Spirit, O, Lord, and for thy precious Word
Your righteousness has come to me, thank you for the Spirit, O, Lord

Your Son bled and died to be the Sacrifice, rose from the dead to reign
Intercedes for us as our true high priest,
    your love is what keeps us fresh
So fill me up, fill me up, fill me up with thy goodness, O, Lord

This fruit of the Spirit is growing in me,
    planted there by the seed of God's word
Rejoicing in the Lord always, thank you, glory to God
So fill me up, fill me up, fill me up with thy goodness, O, Lord

Love is ever-increasing in me, joy fills my inner-man
Peace gives life unto my body, thank you, glory to God
So fill me up, fill me up, fill me up with thy goodness, O, Lord

Patience undergirds my faith, kindness treats others with love
Goodness is the God in me, thank you, glory to God
So fill me up, fill me up, fill me up with thy goodness, O, Lord

Faithfulness means you can count on me, gentleness leaves no room
    for harshness
Self-control lets temperance rule, thank you, glory to God
So fill me up, fill me up, fill me up with thy goodness, O, Lord

Psalm 16 : First Christmas Song

The first Christmas 2,000 years ago, brought Jesus into the world
Born the baby in Bethlehem, Son of God and Son of Man
Unassuming and lowly in birth, yet He brought fire to the earth
Matured and grew up in the Word, to speak out victory assured

Savior wrapped in swaddling clothes, Father's blood inside his toes
Destined to be without sin, the ultimate sacrifice was Him
Trained and taught in the Old Testament
As a preacher and prophet He was sent
This is the Good News of the Gospel: Christ is born

Angels, shepherds and Herod the king; wise men,
     livestock, all should sing
God brought peace and good will to man,
     it's up to us to receive his plan
Mom and dad beside his bed, Father God protecting this lad
The star of Bethlehem heralded the incarnate Word

After 8 days He was circumcised,
     many years later they pierced his side
Shed his blood from beginning to end,
     couldn't stop giving for us to mend
Cradle to the throne this was God's will
King of Kings interceding for us still
The Lord Jesus Christ is the beginning of our life

Born the baby so meek and mild
The One we love, the Great I Am
He grew up and became sin for us
He paid the price, yes, He settled the score
The Son of God, the Son of Man
Born the baby in Bethlehem
The Son of God, the Son of Man
Born the baby in Bethlehem

The first Christmas 2,000 years ago, brought Jesus into the world
Born the baby in Bethlehem, Son of God and Son of Man

Psalm 17 : For God so Loved the World

For God so loved the world, He gave his only Son
To die on Calvary, from sin to set us free
Whoever believes in Him, should not perish from sin
But have everlasting life

He's given us life, more abundantly, He's given us life
From sin to set us free, He's given us life, for hope eternally
His love has conquered death

The choice fruit of our lips, let's give thanks to his name
The sacrifice of praise is what our spirits raise
Thru the Son of God let us offer, the sacrifice of praise

He's given us life, more abundantly, He's given us life
From sin to set us free, He's given us life, for hope eternally
His love has conquered death

Be strong in the Lord, the power of his might
Put on the whole armor so you can really fight
His army's marching on in the victory, his army's marching on

He's given us life, more abundantly, He's given us life
From sin to set us free, He's given us life, for hope eternally
His love has conquered, his love has conquered
His love has conquered death

Psalm 18 : Forgiveness

Awesome forgiveness thru the shedding of His blood
Repentance and confession not misunderstood

We receive the remission of sin by accepting his sacrifice
Brings about transformation, a new creature in Christ

Such love, grace and mercy behind the new birth
The redemption of mankind to those who choose
The gulf of separation has been spanned by the cross
Rebellion of the heart has been dealt with by God's loss

Being reconciled with the Lord is the gateway to life
For our merciful Creator sent Jesus into the world
Our spirit first, then soul and body, nothing missing or broken
It brings to us everything we need that has been spoken

The Father spared not the Son, but released him in the earth
To suffer the penalty of Adam's transgression
Raised from the dead brought about the victory
The war has been won, his mission was complete

So by faith we call it done, heaven is our home
Jesus is our King, with blessings untold
Immortality the future for those who receive
For those who will receive and then wholeheartedly believe
For those who will receive and then wholeheartedly believe

Psalm 19 : Free from Poverty

Christ has set us free from ungodly poverty
A righteous man's reward is true prosperity
Jesus became poor that we might become rich
The blessing of the Lord brings wealth without a hitch

The windows of heaven are open because we are in Christ
Willing and obedient we eat the good of the land
A generous man will prosper as we firmly take our stand
No lack in the Kingdom for we follow his commands

The Lord supplies all of our needs this is true indeed
Food, drink and clothes come from part of our seed
Our Father God gives good things to those who believe
As we ask in faith we are sure to receive

When we sow generously we reap an abundant harvest
So we can give to those in need to help others to succeed
We lend to many but borrow from none this is the Lord's will
We owe no man anything but to love our neighbor still

Christ has set us free from ungodly poverty
A righteous man's reward is true prosperity
Jesus became poor that we might become rich
The blessing of the Lord brings wealth without a hitch

Psalm 20 : Free from Sickness

Christ has set us free from sickness and disease
We do not accept any abnormality
Enjoying good health as our soul is prospering
Abundant life in Jesus Christ thank you, Lord, for the victory

Redeemed from the curse reigning as a king
Overcoming obstacles and any such thing
Jesus came to end oppression that we know full well
He destroyed the works of the devil, we send them down to hell

In thought, word and deed resist the enemy
Receive a long, full lifespan staying strong and healthy
No sickness or disease in heaven, earth is to be a copy
Abundant life in Jesus Christ thank you, Lord, for the victory

We guard our spirit man as part of God's strategy
Renewing our mind and keeping it battle-ready
The body will fall in line for truth shall prevail
We do our part faithfully, remember God will not fail

Christ has set us free from sickness and disease
We do not accept any abnormality
Enjoying good health as our soul is prospering
Abundant life in Jesus Christ thank you, Lord, for the victory
Abundant life in Jesus Christ thank you, Lord, for the victory

Psalm 21 : Free from Spiritual Death

Christ has set us free from spiritual death
The beloved Son gave up his last breath
Eternal life is ours to those who believe
Repentance at the truth gives us the victory

Safe and secure in God's mighty hand
Salvation for mankind is his loving plan
Accepting the work on the cross
So that we not suffer loss
Now and in the world to come

Immortality is our future hope
Abundant life in Jesus Christ
We more than cope
Receiving his divine nature
Puts our name in the book of life
Living forever without sin or strife

Christ has set us free from spiritual death
The beloved Son gave up his last breath
Eternal life is ours to those who believe
Repentance at the truth gives us the victory
Repentance at the truth gives us the victory

Psalm 22 : Fruit of My Mouth

Speaking out blessing with my tongue
No idle or careless words coming out of my mouth
Releasing Godly words is my life's theme
Brings life and health unto my whole being

Only my desires spoken out
Never ensnared with the words of my mouth
Of this I can rejoice and loudly shout
Content and prosperous without a doubt

Lord, you watch over the things that I say
I am enjoying abundance all the way

Blessing not cursing
Coming out of my mouth
This is my right of choice
When speaking with my voice

A fountain of life flows
As I utter truth
Healing is my bread
Because Christ is my head

No such thing as lying or corrupt talk
The tongue is the instrument to write on my heart
Planting good seed for a plentiful harvest
To be a blessing to others with the fruit of my mouth
To be a blessing to others with the fruit of my mouth

Psalm 23 : Gifts of the Spirit

Gifts of the Spirit powered from above
Manifestations come when one walks in love
Desire the greater gifts
To further the Kingdom of God
Blessing others in spite of their façade

Wisdom, knowledge, discerning of spirits
Miracles, faith and healings
Tongues, interpretations, prophecy
These are all downloads of revealing

Baptized in the Holy Ghost this is the start
Yielding oneself fully in the mind and heart
Available and anointed 24/7
So His will be done on earth just like in heaven

These manifestations of power
Only for this hour

Benefiting mankind
To further the Kingdom of God

Gifts of the Spirit powered from above
Manifestations come when one walks in love
Manifestations come when one walks in love

Psalm 24 : Give Thanks

The spirit of thanksgiving, it comes from the Lord
So I give thanks unto the Father of our Lord Jesus Christ
For in the beginning, God commanded his perfect will
Be fruitful, multiply, fill up the earth; subdue it, and have dominion

Jesus was not left in the dark, God spoke out the plan
This unchanging Word, governed the course of his Man
Jesus is our example, we follow his lead
He is the King and the Priest, yes, Abraham's holy seed

Give thanks for the victory in Jesus' mighty name
The fruit of the Spirit in us blesses all who come near
The great Commission command " Go into all the world"
Fulfills the Eden blessing, fill up the earth

Subdue this old planet with the full armor of God on
Victory over poverty, sickness and spiritual death
The world, the flesh and the devil are underneath our feet
We sit with Christ in heavenly places, we have taken our seat

The spirit of thanksgiving, it comes from the Lord
So I give thanks unto the Father of our Lord Jesus Christ
For in the beginning, God commanded his perfect will
Be fruitful, multiply, fill up the earth; subdue it, and have dominion

Psalm 25 : Glorious Love

This glorious love, so inviting
This glorious love, magnificent and mighty
This love of God that's filled with blessings
Never fails, never ends, never condescending

My heart is saturated with love by the Holy Ghost
So personal and intimate, so very up close
Love keeps us refreshed with no fear in sight
Never weighs us down for its burden is very light

God is love, Divine affection
So holy and pure that is our cure
No trouble can separate us from this love of Christ
God sent his Son to pay the ultimate, infinite price

Victorious love, expressed in his love -child
Born a baby, so meek and mild
This awesome love that reigns supreme
A consuming fire that can not, can not be seen

This love of God so motivating
This love of God so captivating
In this dark world, it so constrains us
This glorious love, we must receive, know and believe
This glorious love, we must receive, know and believe

Psalm 26 : God Is Not the Author

God is not the author of sickness or disease
Oppressive trouble comes only from the enemy
We resist the devil with the shield of faith
He flees from our presence and we are kept safe

Speaking to the mountain it must be removed
When we believe in our heart, doubt not our spoken word
As New Testament saints we have the authority
To not accept anything will of God contrary

Who is the god of this world that steals, kills, destroys
Satan thought he was done with the Prince of Life
Resurrection day came forth, Jesus stepped out of the tomb
Ascended up to heaven far above all sin and strife

In thought, word and deed keep the hedge not breached
The wall of protection by angels must be kept indeed
Father God rescues us as we love Him so
The Lord is always with us wherever He tells us to go

God is not the author of sickness or disease
Oppressive trouble comes only from the enemy
We resist the devil with the shield of faith
He flees from our presence and we are kept safe
He flees from our presence and we are kept safe

Psalm 27 : God Is Our Source

You are our source, Lord, of everything
Whatever we need for life and godliness
Received by faith, make no mistake
All the blessings of God they will overtake

Salvation comes by confessing
That Jesus Christ is Lord
Redeemed from sin by accepting his shed blood
Nothing missing or broken in the Savior's love
We're walking, talking, singing out the victory from above

Everlasting life is our new reality
We will never die spiritually
The second death has no power over us
As the righteousness of God we will not suffer this loss

In this life we walk in victory
God, our source, provides abundantly
Faith, hope, love, love, joy and peace
All of the above they will never cease

Wisdom, knowledge and understanding
Come from the Lord
No lack of these in this worldly sphere
For we ask in faith without any fear
Therefore, with God as our source
We can bless without remorse
For generosity it is our course

Psalm 28 : God of Increase

Be fruitful, multiply and fill up the earth
The God of increase has abundance in mind for you
His will is to prosper
For the sake of the Kingdom
By the power of his might
All this is what's pleasing in his sight

Abound to every good work with the grace of God
Your every desire for goodness, He will bring it to pass
Filled with the fruit of the Spirit that will grow and last
Remember that the burden is light
All this is what's pleasing in his sight

We are blessed in our spirit, soul and body
Spiritually, physically and materially
There is no lack in the Kingdom, for the benefit of his children
We are in the victorious fight
All this is what's pleasing in his sight

God's covenant with Abraham brought Jesus into the earth
The Son was made poor on the cross for our fullness
As we share this testimony, we bring glory to God
Our provision is complete by His might
All this is what's pleasing in his sight

Be fruitful, multiply and fill up the earth
With the grace of God abound to every good workBlessed in our spirit,
    soul and body
All this is what's pleasing in his sight
All this is what's pleasing in his sight

Psalm 29 : God of Victory

We turned our back on you, but you never turned your back on me
You are the awesome God who reigns throughout eternity
Our faithful, loving Creator with our best interest in mind
So personal and intimate you are one of a kind

To manifest yourself in this old earthly sphere
You gave us your authority delegated for us here
No doubt about it you need a body
This is mankind's tremendous opportunity

Victory in my spirit
Victory in my soul
Victory in my body
You're the One who makes me whole

As we repent and be victorious
Depending on you for our righteousness
Conquering power from above
You are the God of victory, you are holy Love

Victory in my spirit
Victory in my soul
Victory in my body
You're the One who makes me whole

As we repent and be victorious
Depending on you for our righteousness
Conquering power from above
You are the God of victory, you are holy Love
You are the God of victory, you are holy Love
I love you, you love me, together we walk in victory

Psalm 30 : Hearing

Victory, victory, faith is the victory
Speaking out the Word of God, this is no mystery
Led by the Spirit we meditate on the Sword
Our faith is ever-growing, we are in one accord

Reading, writing, uttering his precepts
Filling our heart with the word of truth
Washed clean by the logos and rhema of his commandments
Sanctified by the truth, our mouth is filled with advancement

Hearing, hearing, faith comes by hearing
Careful listening to what the Word says
Do all the promptings of the Holy Ghost
Walking by faith we are blessed the most

Hearing, hearing, careful listening
Reading, writing, precept uttering
Our faith is ever-growing, we are in one accord
Disciplined with the Word of God
Our mouth speaks out with the Sword

Victory, victory, faith is the victory
Speaking out the Word of God, this is no mystery
Led by the Spirit we meditate on the Sword
Our faith is ever-growing, we are in one accord
Our faith is ever-growing, we are in one accord

Psalm 31 : Heaven

In heaven there is no discord, no strife, only love
No such tears, no such wars, no trouble in the city above
The culmination of blessing is what we long for
The culmination of blessing is when we enter thru heaven's door

No need for the sun, the Lamb will be the light
Crystal river flowing from the throne, no more day to night
Home of the over-comers, we'll rejoice for evermore
Praising God continually, without thirst anymore

In heaven there is nothing to diminish the glory of God
Poverty, sickness and spiritual death are earthly things that will be gone
The enemy has been banished, the curse will be no more
Complete fulfillment comes to us when we walk on heaven's gold
After the 1,000 year reign of Christ, heaven will come down here
God will enjoy his family for the rest of eternity

Remember, in heaven there is no discord, no strife, only love
No such tears, no such wars, no trouble in the city above
The culmination of blessing is what we long for
The culmination of blessing is when we enter thru heaven's door

Psalm 32 : Highest Reverence

The fear of the Lord starts wisdom and knowledge
The fear of the Lord purifies the inner man
It is a life-giving fountain, it blesses the soul
Brings friendship with our God who makes us whole

This highest reverence endures forever
Keeps us from sin a way to sever
Part of the victory the fear of the Lord
Cleans up our act by restraining us all the more

The prophet of God speaks out warning
Chastening us leading to repentance
The fear of the Lord helps keep the veil away
No hardening of the heart we will not be swayed

A doer of the Word, no deception
Seeing ourselves in true perception
From glory to glory shining ever brighter
The fear of the Lord makes the process so much lighter

The fear of the Lord starts wisdom and knowledge
The fear of the Lord purifies the inner man
It is a life-giving fountain, it blesses the soul
Brings friendship with our God who makes us whole
Our intimacy with the Lord will grow and grow

Psalm 33 : Holy Spirit

We were lonely, insecure and full of doubt
Had no power and did not know what to do

But now we're filled with fire by the Holy Ghost
Yielding ourselves to the Spirit of God
Teacher, guide and comforter; inside us forevermore
This was the day of Pentecost he had in store

Speaking out mysteries unto the Father
Heavenly words coming out of our mouths
Edifying ourselves, charging up like a battery
This was the day of Pentecost to set men free

Sealed by the Spirit until the day of redemption
An ever-flowing fountain in our inner-man
Power for witnessing to each and every clan
This was the day of Pentecost that was his plan

We are led by the Spirit in line with the Word
Filled with love by the power of the Holy Ghost
Walking in victory, each and every single day
This was the day of Pentecost for his vessels of clay

Remember, we were lonely, insecure and full of doubt
Had no power and did not know what to do

But now were filled with fire by the Holy Ghost
Yielding ourselves to the Spirit of God
Teacher, guide and comforter; inside us forevermore
This was the day of Pentecost he had in store

Therefore, we are walking in victory each and every day
Walking in victory all the way
Walking in victory, to the very end of the age
Spirit of God living inside us to stay, Spirit of God living inside us to stay

Psalm 34 : I Am Rejoicing

I am rejoicing each and every day
I am rejoicing with Jesus all the way
I am rejoicing with Paul in Philippians
I am rejoicing thru thick and thin
I am rejoicing each and every day

I am rejoicing in the Father God
I am rejoicing in His Son of love
I am rejoicing in the Holy Ghost
I am rejoicing in the living Word
I am rejoicing in the Father God

I am rejoicing with my inner man
I am rejoicing in salvation's plan
I am rejoicing redeemed from the curse
I am rejoicing heaven's unlimited purse
I am rejoicing with my inner man

Rejoicing even though I mourn
Rejoicing when trouble unfolds
Rejoicing for the victory
Rejoicing escaping calamity
Rejoicing for eternity

I am rejoicing each and every day
I am rejoicing with Jesus all the way
I am rejoicing with Paul in Philippians
I am rejoicing thru thick and thin
I am rejoicing each and every day
Rejoicing each and every day

Psalm 35 : In the Kingdom

In the Kingdom there is no lack
In the Kingdom everything's on track
No talk of poverty, sickness or spiritual death
In the Kingdom of our God won't accept anything less

For the Kingdom He sent his Son
For the Kingdom to make us all one
In the Kingdom there is neither Jew nor Greek
We all abide in Jesus Christ with peace and harmony

In this government Jesus is our King
The Word of God is our constitution
We walk in love the great commandment
It's all established in heaven as if in cement

No confusion in this Kingdom
Strife and envy have no place
Set up in our hearts in our inner-man
This Kingdom is heaven on earth as we call for God's plan

Seedtime and harvest is a law of the Kingdom
Sowing first then reaping in due season
Our God gives the increase multiplication
A hundred fold return with faith and consecration

In the Kingdom there is no lack
In the Kingdom everything is on track
No talk of poverty, sickness or spiritual death
Instead filling our mouth with the Gospel which we confess
We won't accept or receive anything less
We won't accept or receive anything less

Psalm 36 : It Must Remove

When we speak unto the mountain
It must remove
As we doubt not in our heart
But believe are spoken word
This we must remember
Not to talk about the problem
But to direct our speech against the foe
Denying it's right to be so

Calling our body healed
Before the manifestation
Brings to us wholeness
A major transformation
Faith is the key which works by love
Nothing in all creation can stop this
Dynamite from above

With the power of attorney to use the Son's name
Satan must bow the knee as we proclaim
Get out, get out, the enemy will flee
A spiritual force has been released
For us to walk in victory

Empowerment comes forth as revelation knowledge flows
Insight and inspiration flood our inner soul
Hearing the word of God triggers our faith to grow
Enlightenment is on the scene and we are made whole

Psalm 37 : It's About Time

Jesus came the first time two thousand years ago
He promised that he would return
And take us to our home
The birth pains are upon us
No doubt about it
This generation will not pass away till all things be fulfilled

The great blessed hope
To those who believe
He commanded us to watch and pray
To escape all these happenings
Then we can stand before the Son of Man
Receive his blessing into the heavenly land

One day with the Lord is as a thousand years
Only two days have gone by since Jesus first came here
His patience is great so that none would perish
His coming will bring great joy to those who wait and cherish

We will marvel at his appearing
Full of power and glory
We'll be awestruck and amazed
Overwhelmed by this story
We cry out with our heart
Come, Lord Jesus, come
We cry out with all our heart
Come, Lord, Lord Jesus come

Psalm 38 : Jesus Comes Again

The second coming of Jesus, that great blessed Hope
Uplifts all his chosen ones with triumphant joyfulness
Jesus was caught up into heaven before the Kingdom came
He's coming back to gather his Saints with awesome splendor
     and fame

With fire in his eyes, crowns on his head
Robe dipped in blood, never to have to come again
The double-edged sword coming out of his mouth
Decimates the deluded ones who followed the Antichrist's touts

Jesus says: "Look, yes watch, for I am coming soon."
Do not be deceived, be vigilant and alert
Watchful and on guard, for you do not know the hour
When He will return with glory and power

The generation that sees the signs will not pass away
Until the heavenly Father has his perfect way
A darkened sun, an unlighted moon, stars falling from heaven
The second Adam fills the sky on that you can rely

Be ready, prepare yourself, do not be caught sleeping
For the resurrection will come suddenly in proper season
Pray to escape the things coming on the earth
To stand holy and blameless before the head of the church

The second coming of Jesus, that great blessed hope
Uplifts all his chosen ones with triumphant joyfulness
He's coming back to gather his saints
Without any spots or taints
No doubt about it, on this you can depend
Jesus will surely, surely come again

Psalm 39 : Long Life

Abundant life in Jesus Christ
Victory in the Lord
Many days on the earth
As we skillfully use the Sword

We shoot for the bullseye
Not to the left or right
120 years
Is what we have in sight

Long life in our consciousness
Each and every day
Thanking God for his goodness
By faith all is okay

On earth be it just like heaven
Good health coming out of our mouths
Speaking only healing
Our desire is what we shout

A long, full life span
Is our hearts intent
Bearing fruit in every good work
We will be content

Abundant life is Jesus Christ
Victory in the Lord
Many days on the earth
As we skillfully use the Sword
Many days on the earth
As we skillfully use the Sword

Psalm 40 : Love Child

Born, He was prophesied from long ago
Born, came at the appointed time
Yes, He was born. Conceived of the Holy Ghost
Yes, He was born. This little love child. He was born

Little love child, with a death sentence on his head
Little love child, Herod tried to make him dead
Little love child, nailed to an ugly cross
Little love child, resurrection followed his grave

Born, born of a virgin girl
Born, then laid in a manger
Yes, He was born, destined to rule and reign
Yes, He was born. This little love child, Yes, He was born

Little love child, suffered in hell for us
Little love child, took our sickness upon himself
Little love child, redeemed us from the curse
Little love child, brought the new, new birth

Born, but no longer a baby boy
Born, satisfied the Father's call
Yes, He was born. To testify to the truth
Yes, He was born. This little love child
He was born.

Prophesied from long ago
Came at the appointed time
Conceived of the Holy Ghost
Yes, he was born. This little love child. He was born
This little love child. He was born

Psalm 41 : Love Your Wife

Love your wife as Christ loved the church
Love your wife as Christ loved the church
Be patient and kind, no harshness allowed
Love your wife as Christ loved the church

Love your wife as you love your own body
He who loves his wife is loving himself
The two shall become one
No division permitted
Love your wife as Christ loved the church

When she asks for things be a cheerful giver
Bless her with love and affection
Be patient and kind, no harshness allowed
Love your wife as Christ loved the church

Husband be the head of this loving team
No division permitted without any seam
Be gentle at all times
Self-controlled and faithful
Love your wife as Christ loved the church

She is an equal heir with you
Be at peace and harmony you two
An unhindered prayer life is a blessing
Love your wife as Christ loved the church

The fruit of the Spirit must be growing
No lack of love in your showing
Ever-increasing, unfailing love
Husband love your wife as Christ loved the church
Love your wife as Christ loved the church

Psalm 42 : Magnify the Word

In chapter 119 the psalmist magnifies the Word
With the logos and the rhema we are fully assured
As we hide God's Word in our heart, sin has to part
Blessed is he who heeds and does the Word

The Spirit of God reveals the hidden things
Revelation knowledge of the Word is what comes in
It will never pass away, so we live by the Word each day
We feast on the Bread from heaven as the Spirit leads

Jesus is the living Word of God
Faith manifests when you listen to it all
Faith from the Word overcomes the world
Blessed is he who heeds and does the Word

The Father speaks and we do well to say the same
Just like Jesus our words are not our own
God's Word will never return empty or void
As we doubt not in our heart for a full reward

God has magnified his Word above his Name
The truth is truth no matter what men may say
Forever settled in heaven, now in our spirit-man
The Word of God contains his holy plan

In chapter 119 the psalmist magnifies the Word
With the logos and the rhema we are fully assured
As we hide God's Word in our heart, sin has to part
Blessed is he who heeds and does the Word
Blessed is he who heeds and does the Word

Psalm 43 : Marriage

65 years of wedded bliss
Striving for, striving for nothing amiss
A man and a woman in full communion
With the Lord waiting for that blessed reunion

Dignity and honor in that marriage state
For a long, full lifespan with the same mate
Together as a team can't be beat
Fruitful to the end without retreat

Two can do more than twice as much as one
How much more when in union with the Son
Walking along hand- in- hand
Companionship so we can take our stand

Pure love shown in abundance
For all to see God's victory
No regrets as we repent
His forgiveness brings about this advancement

In the journey with our spouse
We grow and develop in our house
Into the image of Jesus Christ
Because of him, for he paid the price

65 years of wedded bliss
Striving for, striving for nothing amiss
A man and a woman in full communion
With the Lord waiting for that blessed reunion
With the Lord waiting for that blessed reunion

Psalm 44 : My Heart Rejoices

My heart rejoices, when I am singing, the victory song to the Lord
I can't stop singing, yes singing loudly, for He's worthy on the throne

O, V-I-C-T-O-R-Y-, Yes that is the battle cry, yes that is the battle cry

My loving Father, He listens closely, to every good word that I say
He always answers, in his will, at the right time all the day

O, V-I-C-T-O-R-Y-, Yes that is the battle cry, yes that is the battle cry

The quiet Spirit, He guides us gently, in our conscience spirit true
His interceding, it is a lifeline, for his saints down here below

O, V-I-C-T-O-R-Y-, Yes that is the battle cry, yes that is the battle cry

Cleansed by confession, thru the blood, for each and every sin
Our righteousness, stands complete, by the sacrifice of Him

O, V-I-C-T-O-R-Y-, Yes that is the battle cry, yes that is the battle cry

Yes, that is the battle cry. Yes, that is the battle cry

Psalm 45 : My Provider

Without faith I struggled
Trying to get my needs met
Now seeking first the Kingdom of God
The Lord and I are in step

Every good gift
And no lack indeed
Coming to me in abundance
As I am reaping from sown seed

The King is my provider
Struggling has come to an end
With faith and patience
For God's will can never bend

Victory in my giving
Reaping from what I've sown
Blessing others in word and deed
For giving is what I own

As a cheerful tither
What can I say
The windows of heaven are open
And I can't give it all away

Prosperity and righteousness
Go hand-in-hand
My desires are being fulfilled
As I walk in his commands

Without faith I struggled
Trying to get my needs met
Now seeking first the Kingdom of God
The Lord and I are in step

Psalm 46 : Name Above All Names

Yes, our God is marvelous, mighty and majestic
He is magnificent, the One that we love
Marvelous and mighty, majestic and magnificent
Our eternal God stirs us so

He is the Word of life, and our Advocate
The Word of God, Alpha and Omega
Wonderful Apostle, of our profession
The author and developer of our faith

Jesus is the Way, the Truth and the Life
The blessed Captain, of our salvation
Son of righteousness, and Chief Shepherd
Son of Man and our patient Counselor

Savior and, the Root of David
True Desire, of all nations
Redeemer and Prophet, Prince of Peace and Governor
Sinless Lamb of God and Emmanuel

Mediator and Messiah, Light of the world
Head of the church and our Great High Priest
He is the resurrected, King of the Jews
Lord God Almighty, Lion of Judah, He is the Holy One of the living God

Yes, our God is marvelous, mighty and majestic
He is magnificent, the One that we love
Marvelous and mighty, majestic and magnificent
Our eternal God stirs us so
Our eternal God stirs us so

Psalm 47 : No More Excuses

No more excuses been baptized in the Holy Ghost
Praying in the Spirit in other tongues
Endued with power from on high
No more excuses walking in victory

The love of God in my heart
Speaking out the truth not just in part
The Spirit constrains my tongue
I'm walking in victory
No more excuses been baptized in the Holy Ghost

As I'm led by the Spirit
I speak out godly words
Using the Sword for edifying purposes
Commanding the enemy to flee in fear
No more excuses walking in victory

Gifts of the Spirit evidenced in my life
I am available as I walk upright
No need to cower
We've got the power
No more excuses walking in victory

As I pray in a heavenly language
My inner man charges up like a battery
Empowered and blessed each and every day
No more excuses walking in victory
No more excuses walking in victory

Psalm 48 : No Name

You are my Creator
You formed me in my mother's womb
You did not discard me
In a darkened tomb
You brought me into being
My parents treasured my birth
You placed me in their loving hands
For a long, full lifespan

What a travesty
What a tragedy
What love gone bad
When you end the life of this little lad

When we speak unto the unborn
What will we say
Blessing or cursing
Leaving or stay
Who gave you the right
To end your baby's life

What a travesty
What a tragedy
What love gone bad
When you end the life of this little lad

Repent and be forgiven
Receive a new spirit
Put away the doom of death
Enter into life instead

You are my Creator
You formed me in my mother's womb
You did not discard me
In a darkened tomb

Psalm 49 : Nothing Missing or Broken

Jesus came to make us whole
Nothing missing or broken
We are complete in Christ Jesus
Nothing missing or broken
We've been redeemed from the curse
Nothing missing or broken

Our Father is the God of peace
Completeness, soundness, wholeness
We do not lack any good thing
Nothing missing or broken
His will for us is the best
Nothing missing or broken

We have peace with God through belief in the Son
We are one with the living God
We receive by faith all the promises
There is nothing missing in the Kingdom of God

My body is a temple of the Holy Ghost
I practice his presence, he is the most
He walks, talks and works with me
Nothing missing or broken inside of me

Spirit, soul and body
Everything's complete
I've been born from above
The Spirit is my paraclete

No such separation
No division in sight
We are unified
As the body of Christ

Psalm 50 : Our Armor

The lance of prayer and the sword of the Spirit
Helmet of salvation and the shield of faith
Shoes of the Gospel of peace, breastplate of righteousness
With the belt of truth they comprise our spiritual armor

With these weapons we enforce the victory
That Jesus won for us on cruel Calvary
Resurrection followed the grave
Now it's up to us to proclaim that Jesus saves

First things first, put on the belt of truth
Jesus is the truth, along with his Spirit
Next in line is the breastplate of righteousness
We have right standing with the Father God, no less

Put on the shoes of peace that bear the good news
Preaching the Gospel wherever our feet move
We are always ready to share the hope of salvation
Jesus blessed the world with complete redemption

The shield of faith protects our whole being
Spirit, soul and body, it keeps us from reeling
The helmet of salvation guards our mind and thought life
Protects from the dangers of sin, envy and strife

Sharper than anything is the sword of the Spirit
Speaking out the word of God with due profit
The lance of prayer brings Him into the fray
Triumphant in Christ as we fervently pray

Therefore with this armor we enforce the victory
That Jesus won for us on cruel Calvary
Resurrection followed the grave
Now it's up to us to proclaim that Jesus saves
It's up to us to proclaim that Jesus saves

Psalm 51 : Overcomer

Forgiveness of sin, by faith in the blood
The old man dies, in water immersion
Baptized in the Holy Ghost, the anointing oil
Overcoming through blood, water and oil

With the Word, in me richly
The cleansing blood, washing me white as snow
The name of Jesus, authorizing my prayers
Overcoming through the Word, the blood and the name

The world, the flesh and the devil, must bow the knee
Ever-growing faith, gives us the victory
Jesus is the author, and developer
Overcoming with the faith of God

We follow his example, the anointed One
Walking in the footsteps, of the Blessed Son
He overcame, we must do the same
Overcoming with his authority

Overcoming, with blood, water and oil
Overcoming, through the word, the blood and the name
Overcoming, with the faith of God
Overcoming, with his authority

So, repent and be victorious
Repent and be victorious
You overcoming child of the living God

Repent and be victorious
Repent and be victorious
You overcoming child of the living God

Psalm 52 : People

God so loved people that he gave
God so loved people his will to save
Created in his image nothing left out
Spirit, soul, body that can praise with a shout

A large extended family on the earth
Multiplying and fruitful without any curse
The perfect will of God for his possession
To be one with the Creator by confession

Jesus prayed for all believers
To be unified in Christ
By faith we are receivers
Of his glory and might

What a sight to behold
The church in one accord
Standing before the Father
In front of his heavenly throne

No doubt about it God so loved people
He gave his all to reconcile this world
Holy and blameless, without wrinkle or spot
By the blood of Jesus we have been bought

Down through eternity one big family
Praising God fully in victory
Without reservation or any such thing
Rejoicing before the Lord our Savior King

Psalm 53 : Perfect Will of God

Empowered by the Spirit to do the will of God
Believe on the Name and love one another
Confess Jesus as Lord, acknowledge the resurrection
This is God's purpose for all mankind

To be just like Jesus is what we're supposed to do
In our mind, tongue and actions be ever true
Take captive every thought, guard your mouth with diligence
Bearing fruit with a good and clear conscience

Apply the blood for the forgiveness of sin
Water baptized as a sign of salvation
Filled with the Spirit, anointed with the Holy Ghost
Blood, water and oil is the way to fellowship

Walking in victory to be a good example
Spirit, soul and body a genuine sample
Conformed to the image of the Son of Man
This perfect will of God is his plan

Receive eternal life thru faith in the Son
Healing for our bodies we call it done
No more poverty in our spirit-man
This perfect will of God is his plan

Empowered by the Spirit to do the will of God
Believe on the Name and love one another
Confess Jesus as Lord, acknowledge the resurrection
This is God's purpose for all mankind
This is God's purpose for all mankind

Psalm 54 : Power and Fire

Baptized with power by the Holy Ghost
Consuming fire in our inner parts
Turning our world upside down
For the benefit of those around

Witnessing in every nation
Not neglecting any generation
Fruit of the Spirit manifesting
Love, joy, peace and every good thing

Praying in the Spirit without contamination
Speaking to the Father in his perfect will
As we interpret edification comes
Intimacy with our God will be fulfilled

Power and fire for witnessing
Power and fire for the Christian life
We are not cold nor lukewarm
But hot and fervent for the things of the Lord

Baptized with power by the Holy Ghost
Consuming fire in our inner parts
Turning our world upside down
For the benefit of those around
For the benefit of those around

Psalm 55 : Prayer Song

Talking to my Father, with love in my heart
A never ceasing flow, that refreshes my soul
I am rejoicing, each and every day
As I commune with the One who re -created me

When I pray in the Spirit, Oh, it gets sweet
The perfect will of God, spoken out of my lips
Building up myself, without a doubt
I treasure this relationship that gives me so much clout

Steadfast, constant, be devoted to prayer
When I ask Him for things, He is always right there
Saying "yes" to the promises, written in the Word
I am overflowing with thankfulness, for what I've heard

Watching and praying, is what were called to do
Being alert and vigilant, part of the equation, too
Use the lance of prayer which is part of the armor
So we can stand securely if the tide turns darker

Listen, listen, to what the Father says,
After we have prayed, hear the voice of God
His wisdom is coming, into our consciousness
Giving us the victory in its very fullness

Talking to my Father, with love in my heart
A never ceasing flow, that refreshes my soul
I am rejoicing, each and every day
As I commune with the One who re-created me
As I commune with the One who re-created me

Psalm 56 : Precious

When a Christian loved one dies
There is hope, there is faith
We know that they're in a better place

Jesus died, freed us from fear
Brought life and immortality here
Awake or asleep we're with the Lord
Us believers left behind are not pierced with a sword

When a Christian loved one leaves this earth
Gain is in their future world
Present with the Lord is our hope
Victory is ours we more than cope
Precious is the going home of his saints
Those left behind surely do not faint

When a Christian loved one dies
There is hope, there is faith
We know that they're in a better place

Jesus died, freed us from fear
Brought life and immortality here
Awake or asleep we're with the Lord
Us believers left behind are not pierced with a sword

When a Christian loved one dies
There is hope, there is faith
We know that they're in a better place

Psalm 57 : Priorities

My understanding was darkened
I had no hope in this world
Heart blackened by sin
Until I asked Jesus in

So, I received Jesus as Lord and Savior
Baptized in water
Filled with the Holy Ghost
This is what really matters

Now, rejoicing in the Lord always
Living by faith
Walking in love
Victory from above

Meditating on the Word
Bowing down before the living Lord
No ceasing in prayer
Rousting the enemy from his evil lair

Maintaining the godly armor
Keeping it all in working order
Standing firm when temptation comes
Victory on the battleground

Receiving every blessing
Blessed to be a blessing
Enjoying long life to the full
With the Spirit of God in control

Psalm 58 : Pure and Holy

Pure and holy in the sight of God
For Jesus is our Lord and Savior
His righteousness is ours
Without spot or blemish before Him at his throne
We are pure and holy in the sight of God

No more shame, no more condemnation
Clean in Christ without sin consciousness
No vulgar sin coming out of our mouth
We are mature and complete in the sight of God

No more need to run and hide
From our loving Savior
Fully accepted in the family
Of this we are ever grateful

Iniquity has been removed
Our inner-man made white
Cleansed from within
We shine as sons of light

Given the glory, we are one with Christ
Not unequally yoked, sin has lost its bite
Iniquity has been removed
Our inner-man made white
Cleansed from within
We shine as sons of light

Pure and holy in the sight of God
For Jesus is our Lord and Savior
His righteousness is ours
Without spot or blemish before him at his throne
We are pure and holy in the sight of God

Psalm 59 : Put No Trust in Riches

Don't work for a living
Work for a giving
Put no trust in riches
For God, He is our source

Loving money is a road to evil
Cheerful giving causes no upheaval
Blessing the poor stores up treasure in heaven
God or money, who do you serve?

Be spiritually- minded when it comes to money
Increase is coming this is not a guess
When you sow seeds, you reap a harvest
Multiplication comes in the Kingdom of the blessed

The Father has blessed us with every blessing
Tithing not necessary to earn his favor
It's a joyful expression one to savor
No lack of finances in the Kingdom of God

Streets of gold in heaven, abundance is up there
With the grace of God on earth, we abound to every good work
Seek first the Kingdom, not prosperity
Don't be eager, for restraint is a key

For spreading the Gospel, money is a tool
Hoarding up riches is only for a fool
Generosity imitates the Lord
So put no trust in riches
For our King is the source

Psalm 60 : Quite a Holiday Show

Green needled trees
White glistening snow
Blue Christmas cold
Quite a holiday show
Warm cheerful greetings
Fire places aglow
Soft uplifting music
Yes, quite a holiday show
There is a reason
For this divine season
Celebrate the birth of the Holy One

Smiles from friendly faces
Guests from distant places
Choice food on the table
Singing carols as able
There is a reason
For this divine season
Celebrate the birth of the Holy One

My heart is full now of spiritual grace
For this season reminds me of
The best gift to the human race
This is the reason for this excellent season
Celebrate the birth of our Lord Jesus Christ

Green needled trees
White glistening snow
Blue Christmas cold
Quite a holiday show
Warm cheerful greetings
Fireplaces aglow
Soft uplifting music
Yes, quite a holiday show
There is a reason
For this divine season, celebrate the birth of the Holy One

Psalm 61 : Redeemed

Adam sinned, the curse came upon us: poverty, sickness
    and spiritual death
But Jesus redeemed me from it all, Abraham's blessing makes us tall
Long life, riches and honor are settled in my inner-man
As I meditate on the Word and take my stand

Revelation knowledge concerning the promises of God
Establishes His perfect will for a long, full lifespan
Abundant provision is the standard that keeps us satisfied
According to the riches of our Savior, the Lord Jesus Christ

Prosperity and righteousness go hand in hand
The stripes on Jesus' back heal our every disease
Eternal life is lodged in our spirit secure
As we wait for immortality, which is so sure

Set free from poverty, sickness and spiritual death
None of these in heaven so on earth we can be blessed
Every spiritual blessing is ours to enjoy so free
Sharing all the good things for the rest of eternity
Sharing all the good things for the rest of eternity

Adam sinned, the curse came upon us: poverty, sickness
    and spiritual death
But Jesus redeemed me from it all, Abraham's blessing makes us tall
Long life, riches and honor are settled in my inner-man
As I meditate on the Word and take my stand

Psalm 62 : Reign as Kings

We reign as kings in this life
Thru the one man Jesus Christ
We are children of the most high God
Yet slaves to righteousness
More than conquerors
When we receive the abundance of his grace
This is the victory in Jesus' name

My Lord and my God
The One who reigns supreme
Makes us kings and priests
So we can be a blessing
Just like Jesus in this world
He came to serve and not be served
This is the victory in Jesus' name

Jesus is the author and developer of our faith
Even the size of a mustard seed overcomes the world
When a king speaks out the truth that settles the case
Therefore, we reign in this life for the Kingdom's sake

We reign as kings in this life
Thru the one man Jesus Christ
We are children of the most high God
Yet slaves to righteousness
More than conquerors
When we receive the abundance of his grace
This is the victory in Jesus' name

When a king speaks out the truth that settles the case
Therefore, we reign in this life for the Kingdom's sake

Psalm 63 : Relationship

When I say things unto you, you always listen
When you speak back unto me, I'm in submission
As I ask you for godly things, in your perfect will
The answer is yes and amen for the Kingdom still

I treasure your promptings which come from the throne
Willingly obedient, I will not disown
So personal and intimate to the depths of my heart
Lovingly and firmly you keep me from sin apart

Blessed beyond measure with no end in sight
The God of the universe took notice of our plight
Salvation's plan through the brutal cross
Got rid of the evil, the sinful, cancerous dross

At times I'm corrected chastened by the Word
Disciplined and rebuked for my own good
Back on the path of his righteousness
I'm a child of the living God this is true no less

After the Ascension, the Father sent the Spirit
He comforts and counsels those who will hear it
Sons and daughters of the most High
Adopted into the family we are brought nigh

Psalm 64 : Resurrection Power

Resurrection power burning inside of me
Baptized in the Holy Ghost
Then setting the captives free
Knowing the awesome power that raised Christ from the dead
Available to all who are Spirit led

Received by faith all God has given
In spirit, soul and body for abundant living
Being a blessing to others what we're called to do
With resurrection power that cannot be subdued

Strengthened with might in my inner being
His all consuming fire purifying me
Earnestly seeking the greater gifts
Benefiting others to mightily uplift

Raised from the death of sin just like Jesus
Seated with Christ in heavenly places
Satan far beneath us
Power and authority bestowed upon
Reigning as kings just like God's own Son

Resurrection power burning inside of me
Received by faith all God has given me
Strengthened with might in my inner being
Raised from the death of sin just like Jesus
Raised from the death of sin just like Jesus

Psalm 65 : Revelation Knowledge

Revelation knowledge concerning the promises of God
Establishes his perfect will in the heart of a believer
First comes salvation, then filling of the Holy Ghost
From faith to faith for the rest of our days walking in victory

The righteous live by faith, not sensory knowledge
Just like Adam in the Garden before the Fall into sin
The lady with the issue of blood was moved by her faith
She acted on revelation knowledge and received her healing

Faith for salvation, faith for our healing,
Faith for prosperity, faith for the Spirit's sealing
Jesus is the author of revealed knowledge
When we act on the insight empowerment comes forth

Every Spirit's prompting proceeds from the Lord
All these revelations further the Kingdom of God
In line with the Word they must pass this test
Faith and revelation knowledge are the very best

Enlightenment in the inner-man so we know the power of God
Christ dwells in our heart by living faith so we walk in victory
Always in tune with the Spirit, vigilant listening
Revelation knowledge, acted on gives us the victory

Psalm 66 : Romans Chapter 8

As we walk in the Spirit, we are the righteousness of God in Christ
With our minds focused on spiritual things this is peace and life
Because of his Spirit He dwells in us
Abundant life in Jesus Christ is an absolute must

We are sons and daughters of the living God
Joint-heirs with Christ as we sing out his laud
Sufferings come to all men but glory overcomes
For all the children of the Most high not just some

We wait in hope for redemption of our mortal bodies
Decay will take notice and have to leave
In the freedom of our son-ship
When immortality cleaves eternity awaits us with total victory

Now in this present world the Spirit intercedes
The perfect will of God for us
Which is sure to please

In all circumstances God is working
For the good of his dear children
As we answer his call
We love him and proclaim his wondrous deeds to all
In the presence of sinners to make them tall

No trouble can separate us from the love of Christ
He is interceding for us seated at the Father's right hand
We are more than conquerors which is part of his plan
Nothing can separate us for all of eternity's span

Psalm 67 : Singing Praises

Praises, Praises
We praise the name of the living God
Praises, Praises
Singing praises unto the Holy One

In our praises you live and reign inside us
Our mouth and heart as a team speak the praises of God
Overflowing hope and rejoicing keeps the floodgates open inside
So we offer our praises in faith out of the abundance where you reside

With our close relationship with you, we praise your holy name
A never ending flow that buoys the soul
Blessing the Lord with all of our heart thru eternity
Singing praises unto the living God for all his majesty

Praise be to the Father of our Lord Jesus Christ
Praise to his glorious grace which surpasses our every need
Beautiful praises coming out of our mouth sacrificially
Singing praises unto the living God for all his majesty

According to the Word you inhabit our praises
As surely as Jesus is the Christ of God
So we praise the name of the Lord, we praise the Holy One
Never ending praises for all his majesty

Praises, praises
We praise the name of the living God
Praises, praises
Singing praises unto the Holy One

Psalm 68 : Song of Dedication

I confess Jesus as Lord and Savior
I purpose in my heart to follow your plans
By saying only what I hear the Father say
And doing only what I see him do
Not my will but yours be done
For the rest of eternity

Dedicated, consecrated, committed to walk in all of your ways
I purpose in my heart to follow your plans
For all the days of my long full lifespan

I consecrate myself to you
Surrendering all of what I say and do
I give you my heart, my soul, my mind
My body is your temple so I keep it in line
Whatever you tell me to do
When and where I'm in submission to you

Dedicated, consecrated, committed to walk in all of your ways
I purpose in my heart to follow your plans
For all the days of my long full lifespan

Led by the Spirit in line with the Word
Walking in love filled with the Holy Ghost
Being a doer of the Scriptures
This is what it means to be committed to you
This is what it means to be committed to you

Dedicated, consecrated, committed to walk in all of your ways
I purpose in my heart to follow your plans
For all the days of my long full lifespan
I purpose in my heart for all of my days
I purpose in my heart for all of my days

Psalm 69 : Thanksgiving

Thanksgiving, Thanksgiving
More than just a holiday
Thanksgiving, Thanksgiving
More than family, friends and food
It's a condition of the heart, a grateful attitude
Giving thanks, blessing the Lord, for a most acceptable mood

I'm thankful for the Word, incorruptible seed
Firmly established in heaven, anchor in time of need
Sharp sword of the Spirit, logos and rhema indeed
Mighty weapon spoken out of our mouth that keeps us from calamity

I'm thankful for the blood of the living Lamb of God
Shed for us, now in heaven, never to be spilt again
Receive remission of our sins applying the blood by faith
We've been circumcised like Jesus on day number eight

I'm thankful for the victory in Jesus' mighty name
For the answer is always yes and amen for every Godly claim
We enforce the victory with the full armor of God on
Giving thanks, blessing the Lord each and every new dawn

Everlasting life is what we're thankful for
Spiritual death has been defeated and the curse will be no more
When our physical life is over, stepping into the next world
Immortality consumes us our banner has been unfurled

Thanksgiving, Thanksgiving
More than just a holiday
Thanksgiving, Thanksgiving
More than family, friends and food
It's a condition of the heart, a grateful attitude
Giving thanks, blessing the Lord, for a most acceptable mood

Psalm 70 : The Answer Song

Who, what, why, where, when and how
The Book of Life gives the answers now
The Word of God full and complete
Provides for everything we will ever need

Jesus is the truth made flesh
Suffered and died for us to bless
Arose from the grave, ascended on high
Never to leave us he is always nigh

Gave us the Spirit at Pentecost
Power for witnessing to reach the lost
Redeemed the tongue to speak afresh
Pray the perfect will of God without a catch

As we get into the meat of the Word
Using it wisely as a spiritual sword
Led by the Spirit being a doer
Victory is ours as mountain movers

Who, what, why, where, when and how
The Book of Life gives the answers now
The Word of God full and complete
Provides for everything we will ever need
Provides for everything we will ever need

Psalm 71 : The Battleground

We've got the victory in the battleground of our mind
Taking every thought captive and keeping them all in line
Speaking unto the strongholds telling them where to go
In our consciousness never let up by bringing down every dark blow

We watch and pray over our thought life
Testing every thought and embracing what is right
Not giving negatives any place in sight
Judging every thought and clinging to what is right

Allowing nothing contrary to the Word of God
Clearing all the mountains from this battleground
So that we're not hindered or hampered in any way
With His full authority keeping up the shield of faith

With the sword of the Spirit resist every temptation
To walk victorious in any situation
Keep our garden free from thistles
"As we shoot down all the devil's
missiles

We are triumphant in the battleground of our mind
Taking every thought captive and keeping them all in line
Speaking unto the strongholds telling them where to go
In our consciousness never let up by bringing down every dark blow

Psalm 72 : The Confession Song

I am rejoicing in the Lord always
I am a child of the living God
I am healed, I am whole
Walking in victory and standing tall

I am a joint heir with Jesus Christ
I am redeemed from the curse of the law
Delivered from poverty, sickness, and death
Thus, from the aftermath of Adam's fall

I am more than a conqueror
As I reign with Christ
I am a king and a priest
Complete in his righteousness

I am a blessing as the Spirit leads
Conformed to Jesus' image
My faith is growing this I know
Telling the devil where to go

I am rejoicing in the Lord always
I am a child of the living God
I am healed, I am whole
Walking in victory and standing tall

Psalm 73 : The Creation Story

God started his work creating the heavens and earth
Then released light into this world
He said, "Light be," and it was so
Faith-filled words made it go

He called for sky, land and seas
Seed bearing plants and fruit bearing trees
He called for sun, moon and stars
To mark passing seasons and times afar

He called for birds, fish and animals
Blessed them to fill up the earth
But the best was left for last
He created mankind never to be outclassed

Bear fruit, multiply and subdue
Dominate the lesser living creatures
This Eden blessing is a commandment
For man to follow for his advancement

Adam and Eve created in God's image
Living speaking spirits like his visage
A loving family is the goal
Intimate fellowship with each soul
Communion with our God and we are made whole

Psalm 74 : The Final Judgment

After the thousand year reign of Christ
The White Throne Judgment will take place
The final chapter in the Book of Life
The end result of God's holy grace

What you do with Jesus
Determines your end to come
If you have not repented of sin
Then punishment will begin

Words of sheer terror and fear
Coming into the sinner's ear
One's name not found in the Book of Life
Then cast into the lake of fire

Be warned all you people
Never to wind up there
Embrace the love of Jesus
While time is still in your care

To keep these things in proper perspective
Grasp the Savior's eternal protection
Receive the Lord's awesome redemption
And escape the painful dire of everlasting fire

The Lord's blood has been shed
Then as we confess and repent
No need to have any fear
For God's holy wrath will never come near

Psalm 75 : The Honor Song

Honor the Lord with love in your heart
Honor the Lord with the highest esteem
He is worthy, worthy to be praised
Worshipped and adored for his majesty

Honor the Lord by keeping his Word
It's established in heaven, never to change
As we speak out his truth, victory is ours
By keeping his Word, we honor the living God

Honor comes from fearing the Lord
And loving deeply one another
This essential virtue is a key
For the Kingdom of God to function properly

Honor the Lord by receiving His sent ones
Jesus, Paul, Peter and John
Every true apostle and godly prophet
Honor the Lord by receiving His appointed ones

Honor the Lord with love in your heart
Honor the Lord with the highest esteem
He is worthy, worthy to be praised
Worshipped and adored for his majesty

Psalm 76 : The Last Days

The last days bring about wonder, terror and amazement
Pain and suffering, vengeance and mercy
Unequaled distress, the wrath of God in full display
For repentance and salvation, in the last days

Seals, trumpets, bowls and peals of thunder
All must come to pass before the day of the Lord
If the body of Christ goes thru the tribulation,
The Lord will rescue and protect us from the evil one

Satan, the antichrist and the false prophet
Come to deceive and destroy God's very elect
But they will not succeed for they are bound by the Word of God
This trouble must come to pass but we will remember
     that victory is ours

The Prince of the Covenant is part of the plan
To administrate the church at that present time
David's forces are defeated by the man of sin
And the antichrist is killed only to rise again
He enters the temple and declares that he is god
He releases his wrath only until Jesus comes back again

The second coming of Jesus, that great blessed hope
Uplifts all the saints with triumphant joyfulness
The antichrist is defeated, satan bound for a thousand years
We reign with Christ in the millennium
Until the end of that appointed age.

Psalm 77 : The Love of God

Who can reject the love of God
So compassionate and gracious
Merciful and mighty is our God
Receive the Father's love by faith

In the Kingdom we must forgive
Resentment is out of place
Love your neighbor as you love yourself
Cause Jesus first loved us

The Son of God laid down his life
No greater love than this
Only to rise from the dead
Love took our place instead

In this world seeds are being sown
Faith, hope and love
Listen carefully to what you hear
Invitation coming out so clear

The love of God melts the sinner's heart
To repentance and restoration
Being one with the Lord is the end result
Salvation's what it's all about

God so loved
That He gave
We are called to do the same
Love is ever increasing, we are not ashamed
Victory in Jesus' name

Psalm 78 : The Memory Song

A holy and excellent memory
For all the rest of my days
The Spirit of God reminding me
Of everything Jesus has said

Short-term, long-term and what is between
Not a forgetful hearer
But a doer of the Word
Acting on the fullness of the living Sword

Meditating on what the scriptures say
Speaking out the promises
Is the obedient way
This brings an excellent memory as we do our part
Receiving the mind of Christ is where we can start

A renewed mind is necessary for the victory
This leads to a sound memory
Remembering every good thing
Recalling as the Spirit leads
A thorough recollecting is what we need

A holy and an excellent memory
For all the rest of my days
The Spirit of God reminding me
Of everything Jesus has said

Not a forgetful hearer
But a doer of the Word
Acting on the fullness of the living Sword

Psalm 79 : The New Birth

My understanding was darkened
I had no hope in this world
Heart blackened by sin
Until Jesus came in

Deep-seated repentance
Turned my life around
Confessed Jesus as Lord
Hallelujah! I'm on solid ground

A new creature in Christ
A new species of being
My inner-man has been changed
By confessing and believing

The new birth's not physical
It's hidden transformation
Renewal by the Holy Ghost
Spirit-cut circumcision

The door has been opened
I have entered in
Green pastures, still waters
Peaceful and quiet within

Salt and light are my new nature
Clean and white just like Jesus Christ
I'm blessed beyond measure
With this divine treasure
My salvation's established in his blood

Psalm 80 : The People of God (Part 1)

In the beginning God spoke, "Light be"
Six days of creation and the story began unfolding
In his image God created Adam and Eve
Walking in victory until she was deceived

Adam joined right in and ate of the fruit
The serpent was cursed and mankind followed suit
Sin ran it's course until Noah and his family
The Ark sheltered them all, the chosen dynasty

Time ran it's course and the Patriarchs came of age
Abraham, Isaac and Jacob, the destined lineage
The Father of our faith blessed the human race
Then as a type of Christ Joseph ruled and reigned

Hundred's of years later Moses came on the scene
The children of Israel in Pharaoh's cruel slave machine
Moses tried in the flesh to deliver them
He failed and into the desert he fled

Forty years of wilderness God called out his name
From the burning bush The Great I Am made claim
The Exodus was successful to Egypt's shame
Forty more years of shepherding, mediation was Moses' aim

Trained by Moses Joshua took the call
Victory in the Promised Land, Jericho's downfall
Clearing out their territory step by step
The Lord had blessed his children, the promise had been kept

Psalm 81 : The People of God (Part 2)

Samuel anointed Jesse's shepherd boy as king
Repentance was the theme of David's life of uttering
Solomon followed David as king of Israel
Unequaled wisdom at the forefront until his downward spiral

Isaiah, Jeremiah, Ezekiel and Daniel
Major prophets of the living God in the Old Covenant
Other prophets spoke until the time of Malachi
The last word from God until John the Baptist came nigh

Jesus, Jesus the Messiah came
Anointed by the Holy Ghost, the one and the same
The Father God turned his back on the Son
Only to exalt him to be his ever-living One

Shedding of blood for the remission of sin
Unequaled redemption the sacrifice of him
Everlasting life with eternity in view
Blessed with immortality which will be so new

Peter, James, John and the Apostle Paul
Answered their Lord and Savior's demanding call
Spread the Gospel far and wide
To bless the world with the forgiveness tide

The family of God is multiplying
From Adam and Eve to the end of the age
The will of God is for all to receive
Salvation, baptism and fruitful discipling

Psalm 82 : The Sabbath Song

Rest and worship on the Sabbath day
While in the Spirit abstain from work and play
It is lawful to do good on the Lord's day
Keeping it holy this is part of God's way

Rest and worship on the Sabbath day
It was made for mankind not the other way
Sing and pray to your heart's content
Ministering unto the Lord with full intent

The fourth commandment states very clearly
God rested after creating mankind so dearly
As a pattern for us in his perfect plan
Doing the same for we understand

Rest and worship on the Sabbath day
Communing with our Creator in a special way
Not neglecting the law or any such thing
But following the commandment of Love
Spoken out by our King

Rest and worship on the Sabbath day
While in the Spirit abstain from work and play
It is lawful to do good on the Lord's day
Be blessed keep it holy the Sabbath day
Keeping it holy is part of God's way

Psalm 83 : The Spoken Word

The spoken word from a believer's heart
Heals the sick and raises the dead
For faith-filled confessions carry the day
You can have what you say

When a child of God does not sin with his mouth
By neither omission or commission
Speaking out scriptures with love in mind
The world around conforms to our profession

Victorious living like Jesus
Makes us an overcomer
Controlling the tongue is a key
To walking in his victory

The Spirit of God is the rudder
Directing the course of our life
By not quenching the Spirit
With ugly, perverse strife

Keep the switch of faith turned on
Never speak contrary to the Word of God
For acting upon it is a building block
Our house is built on this solid rock

Use your tongue as a powerful tool
Training yourself in the Gospel school
Blessing others is the rule
Your speech must never sound like a fool

Psalm 84 : The Tapestry of God

The master Craftsman with the loom of time
Creates his living tapestry with love in mind

The redemption of mankind is the theme
Jesus Christ revealed in this color scheme

With threads of faith, hope and love
The rich tapestry grows up above

Every godly thought, word and deed
Is added to the fabric as the Spirit leads

Woven together in perfect harmony
The body of Christ in complete unity

Repenting freely as we confess our sin
Holy and blameless in God's discipline

The people of this world are the object of his love
As He dyes the tapestry with Christ's precious blood

Yes, the master Craftsman with the loom of time
Creates this living tapestry with love in mind

The redemption of mankind is the theme
Revealing Jesus Christ in this color scheme

Yes, the master Craftsman with the loom of time

Psalm 85 : The Truth

God speaks the truth, He cannot lie
He said, "Believe in the Son and you shall not die"
The second death has no power over you
Repent and be victorious, this is what we must do

Our beloved fore-runner Jesus Christ
Is the Way, the Truth and the Life
Let God be true and every man a liar
Surely He delivers us from eternal fire

All is well in the kingdom of God
The Word is established in Heaven above
Our testimony lines up on the earth
His goodness shows up when we speak the truth

The God of liberty has set us free
As we base our life on what we believe
Not on what we feel or see
Our faith in God gives us the victory

Jesus is the Living Truth
His immortality will never change
He is constant, no variableness
Our supreme, everlasting righteousness

The Son, Sword and Spirit are the absolute truth
Nothing in all creation can refute
No doubt about, it's because
Our God is eternal, unchanging love
Our God is eternal, unchanging love

Psalm 86 : The Word of God

The Word of God in my mouth gives me everything I need
As I speak the truth in love, there is no lack indeed
Blessed beyond measure so I can be a blessing
The things that I say line up with the good confession

In thought, word and deed I follow after Jesus
Led by the Spirit he is sure to please us
Yet not our fleshly desires, but his will be done in me
Nothing missing or broken for complete, godly victory

Righteousness and redemption go hand in hand
Following the resurrection so that we can take our stand
Even with the grace and truth of Jesus Christ
We can never pay back the price

Revelation knowledge in my inner man
Birthed from the seed of God's living Word
So that the Father can fulfill his master plan
We are willing vessels in his mighty hand

Psalm 87 : These Three Remain

Faith is ever-growing
Hope is overflowing
Love is ever-increasing, Lord
These three remain and work together for our good

Faith and love spring from hope up above
Faith is the furnace
Hope is the thermostat
Love is the fuel
These three remain and work together for our good

God is love
He has hope
Jesus authors our faith thereof
These three remain and work together for our good

Love is the greatest
Faith works by it
Hope does not disappoint one bit
These three remain and work together for our good

Psalm 88 : This Spiritual Kingdom

Those who believe, belong to a spiritual kingdom
One you cannot see, but for its manifested victory

The Kingdom of God, set up in our hearts
We are complete in Christ, in our inner parts

Now we speak, the truth in love
All is well from above

Spirit, soul and body, nothing missing or broken
Though trouble comes in this world
Our cheerful hearts are more than a token

Framed by words, this spiritual kingdom
Will flourish and blossom when Jesus comes back again

His thousand year reign, in this material world
Brings about peace on earth, for the very first

No doubt about it, the plans have been made
Firmly settled in heaven, to be carried out for our gain

After the White Throne Judgment, Heaven comes down here
No more pain, no more death, no more tears

Psalm 89 : Those in Authority

To keep your conscience clear
To avoid punishment
Don't rebel but do what's right
In the sight of God
Don't bring judgment on yourself
This one thing you can do
Submit to, respect and honor
Those in authority over you

Pay taxes to your government
Give them required revenue
But first of all pray and give thanks
For those who are above you
Bless all your leaders
Intercede and make requests
May there be peace in the land
Under God's caring hand

His perfect will is
That all might be saved
Godly wisdom from our governors
Helps fulfill the Lord's plan
The body of Christ is doing it's part
For those in authority
By fervently praying, asking of God
To bless them abundantly

Psalm 90 : Three in One

Father, Son and Holy Ghost; faith, hope and love;
Righteousness, peace and joy; this is the kingdom from above
Through blood, water and oil we come into your presence
Receiving every perfect gift, Jesus is the very essence

Faith in the Word, the Blood and the Name
Keeps us in peace without any shame
In what we think, say and do; in all our thoughts, words and deeds
With repentance and forgiveness we are walking in victory

Jesus is the Way, the Truth and the Life
He overcame the world to get us out of this plight
Redeemed us from the curse, set us up on high
Seated with Christ in heavenly places far above this earthly sky

Wisdom, knowledge and understanding come from the Lord
Success in every area as we speak with the Sword
With fear and trembling we partake of these three
Growing up just like a strong, solid oak tree

Father, Son and Holy Ghost; faith, hope and love;
Righteousness, peace and joy; this is the Kingdom from above
Through blood, water and oil we come into your presence
Receiving every perfect gift, Jesus is the very essence

Psalm 91 : Triumphant Victory (Part 1)

Words of faith, words of love, words of victory from above
Speaking out good things pleases God as we travel this earthly sod
The mouth is used not for strife my tongue only chooses life

This glorious love, so inviting
This glorious love, magnificent and mighty
This love of God that's filled with blessings
Never fails, never ends, never condescending

In heaven there is no discord, no strife, only love
No such tears, no such wars, no trouble in the city above
The culmination of blessing is what we long for
The culmination of blessing is when we enter through heaven's door

Yes, our God is marvelous, mighty and majestic
He is magnificent, the one that we love
Marvelous and mighty, majestic and magnificent
Our eternal God stirs us so

Empowered by the Spirit to do the will of God
Believe on the name and love one another
Confess Jesus is Lord, acknowledge the resurrection
This is God's purpose for all mankind

Talking to my Father, with love in my heart
A never ceasing flow that refreshes my soul
I am rejoicing each and every day
As I commune with the one who re-created me

Adam sinned and the curse came upon us: poverty, sickness
    and spiritual death
But Jesus redeemed me from it all, Abraham's blessing makes us tall
Long life, riches and honor are settled in my inner man
As I meditate on the Word and take my stand

Psalm 92 : Triumphant Victory (Part 2)

We reign as kings in this life through the one man, Jesus Christ
We are children of the most high God yet slaves to righteousness
More than conquerors when you receive the abundance of his grace
This is the victory in Jesus' name

I confess Jesus as Lord and Savior
I purpose in my heart to follow your plans
By saying only what I hear my Father say
And doing only what I see him do
Not my will but yours be done, for the rest of eternity

Faith is our servant, it is our shield
Victory in this world is like planting seed in a field
With water and sun, the seeds sprout and are grown
Now it is time for harvest and we reap what we have sown

Words are the process starters, they govern the course of our life
Daily conversation is the kindling that starts the fire
Releasing faith-filled words turns the ship around
Because we are living, speaking spirits like the most high God

In the kingdom there is no lack
In the kingdom everything is on track
No talk of poverty, sickness or spiritual death
Instead filling our mouth with the Gospel which we confess

Eternity, eternity, everything pales beside it
The choice you make in this world is crucial to your future inside it
Everlasting life with Jesus or the cruel godless enemy
Choose life with the loving Jesus for the rest of eternity

Psalm 93 : Triumphant Victory (Part 3)

Revelation knowledge concerning the promises of God
Establishes his perfect will in the heart of a believer
First comes salvation, then filling of the Holy Ghost
From faith to faith for the rest of our days, walking in victory

God is not the author of sickness nor disease
Oppressive trouble comes only from the enemy
We resist the devil with the shield of faith
He flees from our presence and we are kept safe

Waves of living glory rolling over me
From faith to faith we walk in the victory
Rivers of living water flooding our inner man
No end to the inundation for the Spirit will never leave

Honor the Lord with love in your heart
Honor the Lord with the highest esteem
He is worthy, worthy to be praised
Worshipped and adored for his majesty

The fear of the Lord starts wisdom and knowledge
The fear of the Lord purifies the inner man
It is a life-giving fountain, it blesses the soul
Brings friendship with our God who makes us whole

In chapter 119 the psalmist magnifies the Word
With the logos and the rhema we are fully assured
As we hide God's word in our heart, sin has to part
Blessed is he who heeds and does the Word

Psalm 94 : Triumphant Victory (Part 4)

Christ has set us free from spiritual death
The beloved Son gave up his last breath
Eternal life is ours to those who believe
Repentance at the truth gives us the victory

Christ has set us free from sickness and disease
We do not accept any abnormality
Enjoying good health as our soul is prospering
Abundant life in Jesus Christ thank you, Lord, for the victory

Christ has set us free from ungodly poverty
A righteous man's reward is true prosperity
Jesus became poor that we might be made rich
The blessing of the Lord brings wealth without a hitch

No more excuses, been baptized in the Holy Ghost
Praying in the Spirit in other tongues
Endued with power from on high
No more excuses walking in victory
No more excuses walking in victory

Therefore, we are walking in victory each and every day
Walking in victory all the way
Walking in victory to the very end of the age
Spirit of God living inside us to stay
Spirit of God living inside us to stay

Psalm 95 : True Faith

Faith is our servant, it is our shield
Victory in this world is like planting seed in a field
With water and sun, the seeds sprout and are grown
Now it is time for harvest and we reap what we have sown

Faith moves the mountains we face in our walk
Overcoming obstacles with power by Godly talk
Releasing faith with every word, then persistence and patience
Keeps us fully assured

Seeing is believing, what most people say
But in God's kingdom it is truly the opposite way
With ever-growing faith nothing is impossible
God never says "no" for we pray in line with the Bible

We walk by faith and not by sight
Thus, we tap into the depths of God's might
Faith for salvation, faith for our healing
Faith for prosperity, faith for the Spirit's sealing

The answer is "yes' and "amen" in the kingdom of God
So be it done, Oh, in the Son
The answer is "yes" and "amen" for all the promises
The war has been won so by faith we call it done
The war has been won so by faith we call it done

Psalm 96 : Unaware

No more consciousness of poverty
No more consciousness of sickness and disease
No more consciousness of spiritual death
Abundant life in Jesus Christ is the very best

As we guard our heart with the armor of God
The will of the Kingdom is taking place
The whole, inner man is kept pure and sweet
Sin consciousness is gone and victory's complete

Toiling for a living is out of step
Working on assignment is better yet
Divine health is what we're calling for
Enjoying life to the full is what's in store

Redeemed from the curse is being mentioned again
Received by faith brings yes and amen
Manifestation comes is what we have learned
So we can rest and be unconcerned

Spirit, soul and body, nothing to be left undone
The Lord will bring us to fulfillment in the likeness of his Son
Heart, conscience, understanding;
    mind, will, emotions; flesh, blood and bone
The Father God restored what the first Adam had known

Redeemed from the curse, received by faith
In the spiritual realm we are kept safe
No consciousness of poverty, sickness, spiritual death
Abundant life in Jesus Christ is the very best
Abundant life in Jesus Christ is the very best

Psalm 97 : Unity

First comes salvation, by the blood of the Lamb
Next, immersion in water, the old man dies before the Great I Am
Then, baptized in the Spirit, filled with witnessing power
Blood, water and oil is the way in this unifying hour

We are one with the Heavenly Father
As Christ dwells in our hearts by faith
Our bodies are a temple of the Holy Ghost
This is no mistake

We've been given the glory, of God Almighty
Enjoying fellowship with the Trinity
The Eden blessing has been restored as we believe
Harmony, not discord, has been received

Father, Son, Spirit and the body of Christ indeed
No division or schism in thought, word and deed
Unified as one walking in victory
Permeated with love is the divine key

First comes salvation, by the blood of the Lamb
Next, immersion in water, the old man dies before the Great I Am
Then, baptized in the Holy Ghost, filled with witnessing power
Blood, water and oil is the way in this unifying hour

Psalm 98 : Victory Song

I'm walking, talking, singing out the victory song, yes, indeed
I'm walking, talking, singing out the victory song, yes, indeed
I love you, Father God, with all my heart, all my soul, mind and strength
I love you, Lord God Almighty, thank you for the victory
The Father, Son and Holy Ghost, I'm walking in your victory
Thru faith in the Word, the Blood and the Name
I'm walking in your victory
Faith is ever growing, hope is overflowing, love is ever increasing, Lord

Jesus, you're my Lord and Savior, healer and deliverer
You prosper me in every area of my life
Filled with the wisdom of the living God, his knowledge and
    understanding
I can't stop singing about you, Lord, I can't stop singing about you
For I'm walking in the victory, over the world, the flesh and the devil
I'm walking in the victory over poverty, sickness and spiritual death

My heart is pure, conscience is clear, I have great understanding
The mind of Christ, an iron will and godly emotions
A strong and healthy body for all of my days
I thank you, Lord, for the victory

Father, Son and Holy Ghost
Faith, hope and love
Righteousness, peace and joy
Wisdom, knowledge and understanding
The Word, the Blood and the Name
I'm walking in the victory in Jesus' name
Everlasting life in Christ, both now and forevermore
Yes, everlasting life in Christ, both now and forevermore

I praise your holy, holy Name
I praise your holy, holy Name
I praise your holy, holy Name
I praise your holy, holy Name

Psalm 99 : Waves of Glory

Waves of living glory rolling over me
From faith to faith we walk in the victory
Rivers of living water flooding our inner man
No end to the inundation for the Spirit will never leave

Power, might, dominion, delegated authority
Kings and priests in this world then into eternity
Divine destination Heaven is our home
Now in the spirit realm then in the material world

The glory cloud overwhelms as we pray in the Holy Ghost
Enjoying his awesome presence rejoicing in the Lord
No need to draw back as we repopulate the earth
From faith to faith and glory to glory Jesus has overcome the world

Waves of living glory rolling over me
From faith to faith we walk in the victory
Rivers of living water flooding our inner man
No end to the inundation for the Spirit will never leave

Psalm 100 : What About Troubles and Trials

Be cheerful in the midst of troubles
Be cheerful when trials come
Jesus has given us his victory
Through delegated authority
When encountering afflictions
Perseverance grows
Nothing missing, nothing broken
End result of this flow

Chastening and correction
Part of our spiritual walk
We are legitimate children
More than just idle talk
Rebuked by the Lord
This is a righteous blessing
Even though not pleasant
Necessary for godly possessing

When persecuted for righteousness
Rejoice in the Lord
You are following after
The prophets of old
Overcomers experience persecution
It comes upon the godly
No need to run and hide
We must live to override

Suffering in this life
Leads to glorification
Nothing on the earth
Compares to heaven's beautification
The glory to be revealed
Surpasses all troubles and trials
Our Mighty God overwhelms every worldly mile

Psalm 101 : Words Are the Process Starters

Words are the process starters, they govern the course of our life
Daily conversation, is the kindling that starts the fire
Releasing faith-filled words, turns the ship around
Because we are living speaking spirits like the most high God

In beginning the Lord commanded:"Let there be light"
Six days of creation and his confessions came to pass
We follow his example, say the desires of our heart
According to the law of faith we do our part

Restrained words are a key to walking in victory
Our overcoming testimony keeps us from calamity
Circumstances come and go but His words will never pass away
Imitating Jesus we speak only what the Father says

Using the Sword of the Spirit cuts the enemy in half
Satan has no hold on us when we utter only words that last
Wisdom, knowledge and understanding come out of our mouth
For inside our inmost being there is no drought

The words of a righteous man are full of power and effectiveness
God makes us mighty in word and deed just like Peter and Jesus
The Lord God Almighty backs our profession to the end
As we confess He is Lord and do not bend

In the Hebrew language words and things go hand in hand
The creative process flows as revelation knowledge goes
Out of the mouth from a believers heart
Yes, you have what you say when you do not doubt

For words are the process starters, they govern the course of our life
Daily conversation, is the kindling that starts the fire
Releasing faith-filled words, turns the ship around
Because we are living speaking spirits like the most high God
We are living speaking spirits like the most high God

Psalm 102 : Years of Glory

Man's days shall be one hundred and twenty years
Enjoying good health in spite of a few tears
Being a blessing to others as the Spirit leads
Abundant life in Jesus Christ, He is sure to please

Long life in this realm can be a blessing
Building up treasure in heaven during this world's testing
Shooting for the bullseye, not to the right or left
A long, full life span by faith we call it blessed

Starting as a newborn down the path of life
Crawling, walking, talking but the end time is in sight
Planning from day one with the finish line in view
A dozen decades later, then eternity so new

No regrets, no unforgiveness in this life so true
Faith, hope and love keep the heart in tune
As my God reigns inside of me
His long life for man prepares for eternity

Years of glory on this old earth
No compromising we've been redeemed from the curse
Long life, riches and honor are settled in my inner man
As I meditate on the Word and take my stand

Psalm 103 : Your Choice

The mystery of a free will
God will not violate
He created you and gave you a choice
To determine your own fate

When you hear the Gospel
Take it to heart
Say yes to the Master's plea
Don't walk away or flee

Accept his gracious salvation
Don't spurn the Savior's love
He has your best interest in mind
And he is patient and kind

Eternity hangs in the balance
Don't let the message fall on deaf ears
When he lovingly calls out your name
Don't kick him in the face

Speak out his name with reverence
Don't reject with disdain or fearful silence
Things can come to a point
Where there is no return
Make no foolish mistake
But let faith awake

Accept his gracious salvation
Don't spurn the Savior's love
He has your best interest in mind
And he is patient and kind

Psalm 104 : You've Rescued Me

O, Lord, you've rescued me, from the darkness you let me see
Your Word renews my mind, lights the path that I can find
Your Spirit comforts my heart, and nothing can keep us apart

Your love is now mine to share for all time, you've given the sign

O, Lord, you gave your life, to set me free from sin and strife
Buried in a rich man's grave, sealed in a rocky cave
God raised you from the dead, to give me life instead of death

Your love is now mine to share for all time, you've given the sign

O, Lord, you've given me, victory thru faith in the Word
Faith in the blood and the name, I'm walking in your victory
For the Father always causes me, to triumph in Christ Jesus my Lord

Your love is now mine to share for all time, you've given the sign

O, Lord, you've blessed me so, that I can generously give and go
Having all that I need, completely satisfied to succeed
Never lacking anything good, this truth is clearly understood.

Your love is now mine to share for all time, you've given the sign
Your love is now mine to share for all time, you've given the sign